50 Taco and Salsa Dishes

By: Kelly Johnson

Table of Contents

- Tacos al Pastor
- Beef Tacos with Salsa Roja
- Shrimp Tacos with Mango Salsa
- Fish Tacos with Cabbage Slaw
- Carne Asada Tacos
- Chicken Tacos with Pineapple Salsa
- Barbacoa Tacos
- Veggie Tacos with Avocado Salsa
- Taco Salad with Salsa Dressing
- Pork Carnitas Tacos
- Tacos de Lengua
- Tacos de Pollo con Salsa Verde
- Chorizo Tacos with Tomato Salsa
- Tacos de Bistec
- Spicy Tofu Tacos with Cilantro Lime Salsa
- Spicy Shrimp Tacos with Avocado Salsa
- Ground Turkey Tacos with Salsa Fresca
- Al Pastor Tacos with Pineapple Salsa
- Baja Fish Tacos with Cilantro Slaw
- Steak Tacos with Roasted Tomato Salsa
- Breakfast Tacos with Salsa Verde
- Taco Bowl with Fresh Salsa
- Chicken and Black Bean Tacos
- Chipotle Chicken Tacos with Corn Salsa
- Tacos de Pescado
- Grilled Veggie Tacos with Tomato Salsa
- Lamb Tacos with Mint Salsa
- Beef and Bean Tacos with Pico de Gallo
- Mushroom Tacos with Salsa Roja
- Tacos with Salsa de Tomatillo
- Carnitas Tacos with Cilantro Salsa
- Grilled Chicken Tacos with Mango Salsa
- Sweet Potato Tacos with Avocado Salsa
- BBQ Chicken Tacos with Peach Salsa
- Tacos de Cochinita Pibil

- Salsa Roja Chicken Tacos
- Grilled Pork Tacos with Pineapple Salsa
- Guacamole and Salsa Tacos
- Korean BBQ Beef Tacos with Gochujang Salsa
- Salmon Tacos with Cucumber Salsa
- Battered Fish Tacos with Chipotle Salsa
- Steak and Avocado Tacos
- Spicy Shrimp Tacos with Pineapple Salsa
- Carne Asada Fries with Salsa
- Crispy Fish Tacos with Spicy Avocado Salsa
- Taco Flatbread with Salsa
- Spicy Chicken Tacos with Mango Habanero Salsa
- BBQ Pulled Pork Tacos with Cilantro Lime Salsa
- Grilled Veggie Tacos with Corn Salsa
- Tex-Mex Tacos with Roasted Pepper Salsa

Tacos al Pastor

Ingredients:

- 2 lbs pork shoulder (thinly sliced)
- 1/4 cup pineapple juice
- 1/4 cup orange juice
- 3 cloves garlic (minced)
- 2 tablespoons achiote paste
- 1 tablespoon chili powder
- 1 teaspoon cumin
- 1 teaspoon paprika
- Salt and pepper to taste
- 1/2 pineapple (peeled and sliced)
- 12 small corn tortillas
- Fresh cilantro and diced onions for garnish

Instructions:

1. **Marinate the Pork:** In a large bowl, combine pineapple juice, orange juice, garlic, achiote paste, chili powder, cumin, paprika, salt, and pepper. Add the pork slices and toss to coat. Marinate for at least 1 hour (preferably overnight).
2. **Grill the Pork:** Preheat a grill or skillet over medium-high heat. Grill the pork and pineapple slices until cooked through and lightly charred, about 5-7 minutes per side.
3. **Assemble Tacos:** Slice the grilled pork and pineapple. Warm the tortillas and top with pork, pineapple, cilantro, and onions.
4. **Serve:** Serve the tacos al pastor hot with lime wedges on the side.

Beef Tacos with Salsa Roja

Ingredients:

- 1 lb ground beef
- 1 small onion (chopped)
- 2 cloves garlic (minced)
- 1 teaspoon cumin
- 1 teaspoon chili powder
- Salt and pepper to taste
- 1/2 cup salsa roja (store-bought or homemade)
- 12 small corn tortillas
- Fresh cilantro and lime wedges for garnish

Instructions:

1. **Cook the Beef:** In a large skillet, cook ground beef over medium heat until browned. Add onion and garlic, and cook until softened, about 5 minutes.
2. **Season the Beef:** Stir in cumin, chili powder, salt, pepper, and salsa roja. Cook for an additional 3-4 minutes, allowing the flavors to meld.
3. **Assemble Tacos:** Warm the tortillas and fill them with the beef mixture.
4. **Serve:** Garnish with cilantro and a squeeze of lime, and serve.

Shrimp Tacos with Mango Salsa

Ingredients:

- 1 lb shrimp (peeled and deveined)
- 1 tablespoon olive oil
- 1 teaspoon chili powder
- Salt and pepper to taste
- 1 cup mango (diced)
- 1/4 cup red onion (diced)
- 1/4 cup cilantro (chopped)
- 1 tablespoon lime juice
- 12 small corn tortillas

Instructions:

1. **Cook the Shrimp:** Heat olive oil in a skillet over medium-high heat. Season the shrimp with chili powder, salt, and pepper. Cook the shrimp for 2-3 minutes on each side until pink and cooked through.
2. **Make Mango Salsa:** In a bowl, combine diced mango, red onion, cilantro, and lime juice. Stir to combine.
3. **Assemble Tacos:** Warm the tortillas and fill them with the cooked shrimp and mango salsa.
4. **Serve:** Serve the shrimp tacos with additional lime wedges on the side.

Fish Tacos with Cabbage Slaw

Ingredients:

- 1 lb white fish fillets (such as tilapia or cod)
- 1 tablespoon olive oil
- 1 teaspoon cumin
- 1 teaspoon paprika
- Salt and pepper to taste
- 1/4 small cabbage (shredded)
- 1/4 cup mayonnaise
- 1 tablespoon lime juice
- 1 tablespoon chopped cilantro
- 12 small corn tortillas

Instructions:

1. **Cook the Fish:** Preheat the skillet with olive oil over medium-high heat. Season the fish with cumin, paprika, salt, and pepper. Cook the fish for 3-4 minutes on each side until golden brown and flaky.
2. **Make the Cabbage Slaw:** In a bowl, combine shredded cabbage, mayonnaise, lime juice, and cilantro. Mix well.
3. **Assemble Tacos:** Warm the tortillas and top with the fish fillets and cabbage slaw.
4. **Serve:** Serve the fish tacos with extra lime wedges.

Carne Asada Tacos

Ingredients:

- 1 lb flank steak or skirt steak
- 2 tablespoons olive oil
- 2 cloves garlic (minced)
- 1 tablespoon lime juice
- 1 tablespoon orange juice
- 1 teaspoon cumin
- 1 teaspoon chili powder
- Salt and pepper to taste
- 12 small corn tortillas
- Fresh cilantro and diced onions for garnish

Instructions:

1. **Marinate the Steak:** In a bowl, combine olive oil, garlic, lime juice, orange juice, cumin, chili powder, salt, and pepper. Add the steak and marinate for at least 30 minutes (or up to 4 hours).
2. **Grill the Steak:** Preheat a grill or skillet over medium-high heat. Grill the steak for about 4-5 minutes per side for medium-rare, or longer for desired doneness.
3. **Slice the Steak:** Remove the steak from the grill and let it rest for a few minutes before slicing it thinly against the grain.
4. **Assemble Tacos:** Warm the tortillas and top with sliced carne asada, cilantro, and onions.
5. **Serve:** Serve the carne asada tacos with lime wedges.

Chicken Tacos with Pineapple Salsa

Ingredients:

- 1 lb chicken breast (boneless, skinless)
- 1 tablespoon olive oil
- 1 teaspoon chili powder
- 1 teaspoon cumin
- Salt and pepper to taste
- 1 cup pineapple (diced)
- 1/4 cup red onion (diced)
- 1/4 cup cilantro (chopped)
- 1 tablespoon lime juice
- 12 small corn tortillas

Instructions:

1. **Cook the Chicken:** Heat olive oil in a skillet over medium-high heat. Season the chicken with chili powder, cumin, salt, and pepper. Cook for 6-7 minutes per side until the chicken is cooked through.
2. **Make Pineapple Salsa:** In a bowl, combine diced pineapple, red onion, cilantro, and lime juice. Stir to combine.
3. **Shred the Chicken:** Let the chicken rest for a few minutes before shredding it with a fork.
4. **Assemble Tacos:** Warm the tortillas and fill them with shredded chicken and pineapple salsa.
5. **Serve:** Serve the chicken tacos with extra lime wedges.

Barbacoa Tacos

Ingredients:

- 2 lbs beef chuck roast
- 1 onion (chopped)
- 3 cloves garlic (minced)
- 2 tablespoons chipotle peppers in adobo sauce (chopped)
- 1 teaspoon cumin
- 1 teaspoon oregano
- 1 cup beef broth
- 1/4 cup apple cider vinegar
- Salt and pepper to taste
- 12 small corn tortillas
- Fresh cilantro and diced onions for garnish

Instructions:

1. **Cook the Barbacoa:** In a slow cooker, combine beef chuck, onion, garlic, chipotle peppers, cumin, oregano, beef broth, apple cider vinegar, salt, and pepper. Cook on low for 8 hours or high for 4-5 hours until the meat is tender.
2. **Shred the Beef:** Remove the beef from the slow cooker and shred with two forks.
3. **Assemble Tacos:** Warm the tortillas and fill them with the shredded barbacoa.
4. **Serve:** Garnish with cilantro and diced onions, and serve with lime wedges.

Veggie Tacos with Avocado Salsa

Ingredients:

- 1 zucchini (diced)
- 1 bell pepper (diced)
- 1 red onion (diced)
- 1 tablespoon olive oil
- 1 teaspoon cumin
- Salt and pepper to taste
- 1 avocado (mashed)
- 1 tablespoon lime juice
- 1/4 cup cilantro (chopped)
- 12 small corn tortillas

Instructions:

1. **Sauté Vegetables:** Heat olive oil in a skillet over medium heat. Add zucchini, bell pepper, and onion. Cook for 5-7 minutes until the vegetables are tender. Season with cumin, salt, and pepper.
2. **Make Avocado Salsa:** In a bowl, combine mashed avocado, lime juice, and cilantro. Stir to combine.
3. **Assemble Tacos:** Warm the tortillas and fill them with the sautéed vegetables and avocado salsa.
4. **Serve:** Serve the veggie tacos with extra cilantro.

Taco Salad with Salsa Dressing

Ingredients (for Salad):

- 1 lb ground beef
- 1 tablespoon olive oil
- 1 packet taco seasoning
- 4 cups lettuce (shredded)
- 1 tomato (diced)
- 1/4 cup shredded cheddar cheese
- 1/4 cup sliced black olives
- Tortilla chips for garnish

Ingredients (for Salsa Dressing):

- 1/2 cup salsa
- 1/4 cup sour cream
- 1 tablespoon lime juice
- Salt and pepper to taste

Instructions:

1. **Cook the Beef:** Heat olive oil in a skillet over medium heat. Cook the ground beef until browned, then stir in taco seasoning and cook according to package instructions.
2. **Make Salsa Dressing:** In a small bowl, combine salsa, sour cream, lime juice, salt, and pepper. Mix well.
3. **Assemble Salad:** In a large bowl, combine lettuce, tomato, cheese, olives, and taco beef. Drizzle with salsa dressing and toss to coat.
4. **Serve:** Top with tortilla chips for crunch and serve.

Pork Carnitas Tacos

Ingredients:

- 2 lbs pork shoulder (cut into large chunks)
- 1 onion (quartered)
- 4 cloves garlic (smashed)
- 1 orange (cut in half)
- 2 teaspoons cumin
- 1 teaspoon oregano
- 1/2 teaspoon chili powder
- Salt and pepper to taste
- 1/4 cup cilantro (chopped)
- 12 small corn tortillas

Instructions:

1. **Cook the Pork:** In a slow cooker, add the pork shoulder, onion, garlic, orange halves, cumin, oregano, chili powder, salt, and pepper. Cover with water and cook on low for 6-8 hours, or until the pork is tender and easily shreds.
2. **Shred the Pork:** Remove the pork from the slow cooker and shred it using two forks.
3. **Crisp the Carnitas:** Preheat a skillet over medium-high heat. Add the shredded pork and cook for 5-7 minutes until crispy on the edges.
4. **Assemble Tacos:** Warm the tortillas and fill them with the crispy carnitas. Garnish with chopped cilantro.
5. **Serve:** Serve the carnitas tacos with lime wedges on the side.

Tacos de Lengua (Beef Tongue Tacos)

Ingredients:

- 2 lbs beef tongue
- 1 onion (quartered)
- 3 cloves garlic (smashed)
- 2 bay leaves
- 1 teaspoon cumin
- Salt and pepper to taste
- 12 small corn tortillas
- 1/4 cup cilantro (chopped)
- 1/2 cup salsa (your choice)

Instructions:

1. **Cook the Beef Tongue:** In a large pot, add beef tongue, onion, garlic, bay leaves, cumin, salt, and pepper. Cover with water and simmer for 2-3 hours until the tongue is tender.
2. **Peel and Shred the Tongue:** Remove the tongue from the pot, let it cool slightly, then peel off the tough outer skin. Shred the meat with a fork.
3. **Assemble Tacos:** Warm the tortillas and fill them with the shredded beef tongue. Top with cilantro and your choice of salsa.
4. **Serve:** Serve the tacos de lengua with extra salsa on the side.

Tacos de Pollo con Salsa Verde (Chicken Tacos with Green Salsa)

Ingredients:

- 2 lbs chicken breasts (boneless, skinless)
- 1 tablespoon olive oil
- 1 teaspoon cumin
- 1 teaspoon paprika
- Salt and pepper to taste
- 1 cup salsa verde (store-bought or homemade)
- 12 small corn tortillas
- 1/4 cup cilantro (chopped)
- Lime wedges for garnish

Instructions:

1. **Cook the Chicken:** Heat olive oil in a skillet over medium-high heat. Season the chicken with cumin, paprika, salt, and pepper. Cook the chicken for 5-6 minutes per side until browned and cooked through.
2. **Shred the Chicken:** Remove the chicken from the skillet and shred it using two forks.
3. **Add Salsa Verde:** Return the shredded chicken to the skillet, pour in salsa verde, and cook for an additional 2-3 minutes to warm through.
4. **Assemble Tacos:** Warm the tortillas and fill them with the chicken mixture.
5. **Serve:** Garnish with cilantro and serve with lime wedges.

Chorizo Tacos with Tomato Salsa

Ingredients:

- 1 lb chorizo sausage (removed from casing)
- 1 small onion (diced)
- 2 cloves garlic (minced)
- 2 tomatoes (diced)
- 1/4 cup cilantro (chopped)
- 1 tablespoon lime juice
- 12 small corn tortillas

Instructions:

1. **Cook the Chorizo:** In a skillet over medium heat, cook the chorizo, breaking it up with a spoon until browned and fully cooked, about 6-7 minutes.
2. **Make Tomato Salsa:** In a bowl, combine diced tomatoes, cilantro, and lime juice. Stir to combine.
3. **Assemble Tacos:** Warm the tortillas and fill them with cooked chorizo. Top with tomato salsa.
4. **Serve:** Serve the chorizo tacos with extra lime wedges.

Tacos de Bistec (Steak Tacos)

Ingredients:

- 1 lb flank steak or skirt steak
- 1 tablespoon olive oil
- 1 teaspoon chili powder
- 1 teaspoon cumin
- Salt and pepper to taste
- 1 onion (diced)
- 1/4 cup cilantro (chopped)
- 12 small corn tortillas

Instructions:

1. **Cook the Steak:** Preheat a grill or skillet over medium-high heat. Season the steak with chili powder, cumin, salt, and pepper. Grill for 4-5 minutes per side for medium-rare, or longer for desired doneness.
2. **Slice the Steak:** Let the steak rest for 5 minutes, then slice thinly against the grain.
3. **Assemble Tacos:** Warm the tortillas and fill them with sliced steak, onion, and cilantro.
4. **Serve:** Serve with lime wedges and extra cilantro.

Spicy Tofu Tacos with Cilantro Lime Salsa

Ingredients:

- 1 block firm tofu (pressed and cubed)
- 1 tablespoon olive oil
- 1 teaspoon chili powder
- 1/2 teaspoon cumin
- Salt and pepper to taste
- 1/4 cup cilantro (chopped)
- 1 tablespoon lime juice
- 1/2 cup salsa (your choice)
- 12 small corn tortillas

Instructions:

1. **Cook the Tofu:** Heat olive oil in a skillet over medium-high heat. Add cubed tofu and cook until crispy, about 7-8 minutes, stirring occasionally. Season with chili powder, cumin, salt, and pepper.
2. **Make Cilantro Lime Salsa:** In a small bowl, combine cilantro, lime juice, and salsa.
3. **Assemble Tacos:** Warm the tortillas and fill them with the crispy tofu. Top with cilantro lime salsa.
4. **Serve:** Serve with extra lime wedges.

Spicy Shrimp Tacos with Avocado Salsa

Ingredients:

- 1 lb shrimp (peeled and deveined)
- 1 tablespoon olive oil
- 1 teaspoon chili powder
- 1/2 teaspoon paprika
- Salt and pepper to taste
- 1 avocado (diced)
- 1/4 cup red onion (diced)
- 1/4 cup cilantro (chopped)
- 1 tablespoon lime juice
- 12 small corn tortillas

Instructions:

1. **Cook the Shrimp:** Heat olive oil in a skillet over medium-high heat. Add shrimp and season with chili powder, paprika, salt, and pepper. Cook for 2-3 minutes on each side until pink and cooked through.
2. **Make Avocado Salsa:** In a bowl, combine diced avocado, red onion, cilantro, and lime juice. Stir to combine.
3. **Assemble Tacos:** Warm the tortillas and fill them with cooked shrimp and avocado salsa.
4. **Serve:** Serve with extra lime wedges.

Ground Turkey Tacos with Salsa Fresca

Ingredients:

- 1 lb ground turkey
- 1 tablespoon olive oil
- 1 teaspoon cumin
- 1 teaspoon chili powder
- Salt and pepper to taste
- 1/2 cup tomatoes (diced)
- 1/4 cup red onion (diced)
- 1/4 cup cilantro (chopped)
- 1 tablespoon lime juice
- 12 small corn tortillas

Instructions:

1. **Cook the Ground Turkey:** Heat olive oil in a skillet over medium-high heat. Add ground turkey and cook until browned, breaking it up with a spoon. Season with cumin, chili powder, salt, and pepper.
2. **Make Salsa Fresca:** In a small bowl, combine diced tomatoes, red onion, cilantro, and lime juice. Stir to combine.
3. **Assemble Tacos:** Warm the tortillas and fill them with the ground turkey. Top with salsa fresca.
4. **Serve:** Serve with extra lime wedges.

Al Pastor Tacos with Pineapple Salsa

Ingredients:

- 2 lbs pork shoulder (thinly sliced)
- 1/4 cup pineapple juice
- 1/4 cup orange juice
- 3 cloves garlic (minced)
- 2 tablespoons achiote paste
- 1 tablespoon chili powder
- 1 teaspoon cumin
- Salt and pepper to taste
- 1/2 pineapple (peeled and sliced)
- 12 small corn tortillas
- Fresh cilantro and diced onions for garnish

Instructions:

1. **Marinate the Pork:** In a large bowl, combine pineapple juice, orange juice, garlic, achiote paste, chili powder, cumin, salt, and pepper. Add the pork slices and toss to coat. Marinate for at least 1 hour (preferably overnight).
2. **Grill the Pork:** Preheat a grill or skillet over medium-high heat. Grill the pork and pineapple slices until cooked through and lightly charred, about 5-7 minutes per side.
3. **Assemble Tacos:** Slice the grilled pork and pineapple. Warm the tortillas and top with pork, pineapple salsa (made from grilled pineapple, cilantro, and lime), and fresh cilantro.
4. **Serve:** Serve the tacos with extra lime wedges.

Baja Fish Tacos with Cilantro Slaw

Ingredients:

- 1 lb white fish fillets (such as cod or tilapia)
- 1 tablespoon olive oil
- 1 teaspoon paprika
- 1/2 teaspoon cumin
- Salt and pepper to taste
- 1/2 cup cabbage (shredded)
- 1/4 cup cilantro (chopped)
- 1/4 cup mayonnaise
- 1 tablespoon lime juice
- 12 small corn tortillas
- 1 avocado (sliced)
- Lime wedges for garnish

Instructions:

1. **Cook the Fish:** Preheat a grill or skillet over medium heat. Season the fish fillets with olive oil, paprika, cumin, salt, and pepper. Cook for 3-4 minutes per side, until the fish is tender and flakes easily.
2. **Make the Cilantro Slaw:** In a bowl, combine shredded cabbage, chopped cilantro, mayonnaise, and lime juice. Toss to combine.
3. **Assemble Tacos:** Warm the tortillas and fill them with the grilled fish. Top with cilantro slaw, sliced avocado, and a squeeze of lime.
4. **Serve:** Serve the Baja fish tacos with extra lime wedges.

Steak Tacos with Roasted Tomato Salsa

Ingredients:

- 1 lb flank steak
- 1 tablespoon olive oil
- 1 teaspoon chili powder
- Salt and pepper to taste
- 1 cup tomatoes (roasted and chopped)
- 1/4 cup red onion (diced)
- 1/4 cup cilantro (chopped)
- 1 tablespoon lime juice
- 12 small corn tortillas

Instructions:

1. **Cook the Steak:** Preheat a grill or skillet over medium-high heat. Season the steak with olive oil, chili powder, salt, and pepper. Grill for 4-5 minutes per side for medium-rare or longer for desired doneness.
2. **Make the Roasted Tomato Salsa:** Roast tomatoes in the oven until soft and slightly charred, about 10-12 minutes at 400°F. Chop and combine with red onion, cilantro, and lime juice.
3. **Assemble Tacos:** Let the steak rest for 5 minutes, then slice thinly against the grain. Warm the tortillas and fill them with sliced steak and roasted tomato salsa.
4. **Serve:** Serve the tacos with extra lime wedges.

Breakfast Tacos with Salsa Verde

Ingredients:

- 4 eggs (scrambled)
- 1/2 cup cooked bacon (crumbled)
- 1/4 cup cheddar cheese (shredded)
- 1/4 cup salsa verde
- 12 small flour tortillas

Instructions:

1. **Cook the Eggs:** Scramble the eggs in a skillet over medium heat until cooked through.
2. **Assemble Tacos:** Warm the tortillas and fill them with scrambled eggs, crumbled bacon, and shredded cheese.
3. **Top with Salsa Verde:** Spoon salsa verde over the tacos.
4. **Serve:** Serve with extra salsa verde on the side.

Taco Bowl with Fresh Salsa

Ingredients:

- 2 cups cooked rice (brown or white)
- 1 lb ground beef or chicken
- 1 teaspoon cumin
- 1 teaspoon chili powder
- Salt and pepper to taste
- 1 cup black beans (cooked or canned)
- 1/2 cup corn kernels (fresh or frozen)
- 1 cup fresh salsa (tomato, onion, cilantro, lime)
- 1 avocado (sliced)
- 1/4 cup shredded cheese
- Lime wedges for garnish

Instructions:

1. **Cook the Meat:** In a skillet, cook ground beef or chicken with cumin, chili powder, salt, and pepper until browned and fully cooked.
2. **Assemble the Bowl:** In a bowl, layer the cooked rice, ground meat, black beans, corn, and fresh salsa.
3. **Top with Toppings:** Add sliced avocado, shredded cheese, and a squeeze of lime juice.
4. **Serve:** Serve the taco bowl with additional salsa and lime wedges.

Chicken and Black Bean Tacos

Ingredients:

- 2 chicken breasts (boneless, skinless)
- 1 tablespoon olive oil
- 1 teaspoon cumin
- 1 teaspoon paprika
- Salt and pepper to taste
- 1 cup black beans (cooked or canned)
- 12 small corn tortillas
- 1/4 cup cilantro (chopped)
- 1/4 cup sour cream

Instructions:

1. **Cook the Chicken:** Season the chicken with olive oil, cumin, paprika, salt, and pepper. Grill or sauté the chicken for 6-8 minutes per side until fully cooked.
2. **Shred the Chicken:** Let the chicken rest for a few minutes, then shred it with two forks.
3. **Assemble Tacos:** Warm the tortillas and fill them with shredded chicken and black beans.
4. **Top with Sour Cream and Cilantro:** Garnish with sour cream and chopped cilantro.
5. **Serve:** Serve the tacos with extra lime wedges.

Chipotle Chicken Tacos with Corn Salsa

Ingredients:

- 2 chicken breasts (boneless, skinless)
- 1 tablespoon chipotle chili powder
- 1 teaspoon cumin
- Salt and pepper to taste
- 1 cup corn kernels (fresh or frozen)
- 1/4 cup red onion (diced)
- 1/4 cup cilantro (chopped)
- 1 tablespoon lime juice
- 12 small corn tortillas

Instructions:

1. **Cook the Chicken:** Season the chicken with chipotle chili powder, cumin, salt, and pepper. Grill or sauté the chicken for 6-8 minutes per side until fully cooked.
2. **Make the Corn Salsa:** In a bowl, combine corn kernels, red onion, cilantro, and lime juice.
3. **Assemble Tacos:** Warm the tortillas and fill them with sliced chipotle chicken. Top with corn salsa.
4. **Serve:** Serve with extra lime wedges.

Tacos de Pescado (Fish Tacos)

Ingredients:

- 1 lb white fish fillets (such as cod or tilapia)
- 1 tablespoon olive oil
- 1 teaspoon cumin
- 1 teaspoon paprika
- Salt and pepper to taste
- 1/2 cup cabbage (shredded)
- 1/4 cup cilantro (chopped)
- 1 tablespoon lime juice
- 12 small corn tortillas
- Lime wedges for garnish

Instructions:

1. **Cook the Fish:** Preheat a grill or skillet over medium heat. Season the fish fillets with olive oil, cumin, paprika, salt, and pepper. Cook for 3-4 minutes per side, until the fish is tender and flakes easily.
2. **Make the Cabbage Slaw:** In a bowl, combine shredded cabbage, cilantro, and lime juice.
3. **Assemble Tacos:** Warm the tortillas and fill them with the grilled fish. Top with cabbage slaw.
4. **Serve:** Serve the fish tacos with extra lime wedges.

Grilled Veggie Tacos with Tomato Salsa

Ingredients:

- 1 zucchini (sliced)
- 1 bell pepper (sliced)
- 1 onion (sliced)
- 1 tablespoon olive oil
- Salt and pepper to taste
- 1 cup fresh tomato salsa
- 12 small corn tortillas

Instructions:

1. **Grill the Veggies:** Preheat a grill or grill pan over medium-high heat. Toss the sliced zucchini, bell pepper, and onion with olive oil, salt, and pepper. Grill the veggies for 4-5 minutes until tender and slightly charred.
2. **Assemble Tacos:** Warm the tortillas and fill them with the grilled veggies.
3. **Top with Salsa:** Spoon fresh tomato salsa over the veggies.
4. **Serve:** Serve with a sprinkle of cilantro.

Lamb Tacos with Mint Salsa

Ingredients:

- 1 lb ground lamb
- 1 tablespoon olive oil
- 1 teaspoon cumin
- 1 teaspoon cinnamon
- Salt and pepper to taste
- 1/2 cup fresh mint (chopped)
- 1 tablespoon lime juice
- 12 small corn tortillas

Instructions:

1. **Cook the Lamb:** Heat olive oil in a skillet over medium-high heat. Add ground lamb and cook until browned, breaking it up with a spoon. Season with cumin, cinnamon, salt, and pepper.
2. **Make Mint Salsa:** In a small bowl, combine chopped mint and lime juice.
3. **Assemble Tacos:** Warm the tortillas and fill them with cooked lamb.
4. **Top with Mint Salsa:** Spoon the mint salsa over the lamb.
5. **Serve:** Serve with extra lime wedges.

Beef and Bean Tacos with Pico de Gallo

Ingredients:

- 1 lb ground beef
- 1 can black beans (rinsed and drained)
- 1 teaspoon chili powder
- 1 teaspoon cumin
- Salt and pepper to taste
- 1/2 cup pico de gallo (tomatoes, onion, cilantro, lime)
- 12 small corn tortillas

Instructions:

1. **Cook the Beef:** In a skillet, cook ground beef with chili powder, cumin, salt, and pepper until browned.
2. **Add the Beans:** Stir in black beans and cook for an additional 2-3 minutes.
3. **Assemble Tacos:** Warm the tortillas and fill them with beef and bean mixture.
4. **Top with Pico de Gallo:** Spoon pico de gallo over the tacos.
5. **Serve:** Serve with extra lime wedges.

Mushroom Tacos with Salsa Roja

Ingredients:

- 1 lb mushrooms (such as cremini or portobello), sliced
- 1 tablespoon olive oil
- 1 teaspoon cumin
- 1 teaspoon paprika
- Salt and pepper to taste
- 1 cup salsa roja
- 12 small corn tortillas
- 1/4 cup cilantro (chopped)
- Lime wedges for garnish

Instructions:

1. **Cook the Mushrooms:** Heat olive oil in a skillet over medium heat. Add sliced mushrooms and cook for 5-7 minutes until tender and browned. Season with cumin, paprika, salt, and pepper.
2. **Warm the Tortillas:** Heat tortillas on a griddle or in a dry skillet for about 30 seconds on each side.
3. **Assemble the Tacos:** Fill each tortilla with the cooked mushrooms and top with salsa roja.
4. **Serve:** Garnish with chopped cilantro and serve with lime wedges.

Tacos with Salsa de Tomatillo

Ingredients:

- 1 lb chicken breast or thighs, grilled and sliced
- 1 cup salsa de tomatillo (roasted tomatillos, onion, cilantro, lime)
- 12 small corn tortillas
- 1/2 cup lettuce or cabbage (shredded)
- 1/4 cup queso fresco (crumbled)
- Lime wedges for garnish

Instructions:

1. **Prepare the Chicken:** Grill the chicken breasts or thighs and slice thinly.
2. **Warm the Tortillas:** Heat the tortillas on a dry skillet or griddle.
3. **Assemble the Tacos:** Fill each tortilla with sliced chicken, top with salsa de tomatillo, and add shredded lettuce or cabbage.
4. **Serve:** Garnish with crumbled queso fresco and serve with lime wedges.

Carnitas Tacos with Cilantro Salsa

Ingredients:

- 2 lbs pork shoulder (slow-cooked or braised)
- 1 tablespoon olive oil
- Salt and pepper to taste
- 1 cup cilantro salsa (cilantro, lime juice, jalapeño, onion, garlic)
- 12 small corn tortillas
- Lime wedges for garnish

Instructions:

1. **Prepare the Carnitas:** Slow-cook or braise pork shoulder until tender. Shred the meat with two forks.
2. **Warm the Tortillas:** Heat tortillas on a griddle or skillet.
3. **Assemble the Tacos:** Fill tortillas with shredded carnitas and top with cilantro salsa.
4. **Serve:** Garnish with lime wedges and additional cilantro if desired.

Grilled Chicken Tacos with Mango Salsa

Ingredients:

- 2 chicken breasts (boneless, skinless)
- 1 tablespoon olive oil
- 1 teaspoon chili powder
- 1/2 teaspoon cumin
- Salt and pepper to taste
- 1 cup mango salsa (mango, red onion, cilantro, lime)
- 12 small corn tortillas

Instructions:

1. **Grill the Chicken:** Season chicken breasts with olive oil, chili powder, cumin, salt, and pepper. Grill for 6-8 minutes on each side until cooked through.
2. **Prepare the Mango Salsa:** Combine diced mango, red onion, chopped cilantro, and lime juice in a bowl.
3. **Assemble the Tacos:** Slice grilled chicken and fill tortillas with chicken slices and mango salsa.
4. **Serve:** Serve with lime wedges.

Sweet Potato Tacos with Avocado Salsa

Ingredients:

- 2 medium sweet potatoes (peeled and cubed)
- 1 tablespoon olive oil
- Salt and pepper to taste
- 1 avocado (diced)
- 1/2 cup red onion (diced)
- 1/4 cup cilantro (chopped)
- 1 tablespoon lime juice
- 12 small corn tortillas

Instructions:

1. **Cook the Sweet Potatoes:** Preheat the oven to 400°F. Toss the cubed sweet potatoes with olive oil, salt, and pepper. Roast for 20-25 minutes until tender.
2. **Prepare the Avocado Salsa:** In a bowl, combine diced avocado, red onion, cilantro, and lime juice.
3. **Assemble the Tacos:** Warm the tortillas and fill them with roasted sweet potatoes. Top with avocado salsa.
4. **Serve:** Serve with extra lime wedges.

BBQ Chicken Tacos with Peach Salsa

Ingredients:

- 2 chicken breasts (boneless, skinless)
- 1/2 cup barbecue sauce
- 1 cup peach salsa (peach, red onion, cilantro, lime)
- 12 small corn tortillas

Instructions:

1. **Prepare the Chicken:** Grill or bake the chicken breasts. Brush with barbecue sauce during the last 5 minutes of cooking.
2. **Prepare the Peach Salsa:** Combine diced peaches, red onion, cilantro, and lime juice in a bowl.
3. **Assemble the Tacos:** Slice the cooked chicken and fill tortillas with chicken and top with peach salsa.
4. **Serve:** Serve with extra barbecue sauce and lime wedges.

Tacos de Cochinita Pibil

Ingredients:

- 2 lbs pork shoulder
- 2 tablespoons achiote paste
- 1/2 cup orange juice
- 1 tablespoon lime juice
- 1 teaspoon cumin
- 1 onion (sliced)
- 1 tablespoon olive oil
- 12 small corn tortillas
- Pickled red onions for garnish

Instructions:

1. **Prepare the Pork:** Slow-cook or braise pork shoulder with achiote paste, orange juice, lime juice, and cumin until tender. Shred the meat.
2. **Warm the Tortillas:** Heat tortillas in a dry skillet or on a griddle.
3. **Assemble the Tacos:** Fill tortillas with shredded cochinita pibil and top with pickled red onions.
4. **Serve:** Garnish with extra lime wedges and cilantro.

Salsa Roja Chicken Tacos

Ingredients:

- 2 chicken breasts (boneless, skinless)
- 1 cup salsa roja
- 12 small corn tortillas
- 1/4 cup cilantro (chopped)
- Lime wedges for garnish

Instructions:

1. **Cook the Chicken:** Grill or sauté the chicken breasts until cooked through. Shred the chicken.
2. **Heat the Salsa:** Heat salsa roja in a small pan until warm.
3. **Assemble the Tacos:** Fill tortillas with shredded chicken and spoon salsa roja over the top.
4. **Serve:** Garnish with chopped cilantro and lime wedges.

Grilled Pork Tacos with Pineapple Salsa

Ingredients:

- 1 lb pork tenderloin
- 1 tablespoon olive oil
- 1 teaspoon cumin
- 1/2 teaspoon paprika
- Salt and pepper to taste
- 1 cup pineapple salsa (pineapple, red onion, cilantro, lime)
- 12 small corn tortillas

Instructions:

1. **Grill the Pork:** Season the pork tenderloin with olive oil, cumin, paprika, salt, and pepper. Grill for 6-8 minutes per side until cooked through.
2. **Prepare the Pineapple Salsa:** In a bowl, combine diced pineapple, red onion, cilantro, and lime juice.
3. **Assemble the Tacos:** Slice the grilled pork and fill tortillas with pork slices and pineapple salsa.
4. **Serve:** Serve with extra lime wedges.

Guacamole and Salsa Tacos

Ingredients:

- 2 ripe avocados
- 1/2 cup red onion (finely diced)
- 1 lime (juiced)
- 1 tablespoon cilantro (chopped)
- 1 cup salsa (your choice of salsa, fresh or store-bought)
- 12 small corn tortillas
- Salt and pepper to taste

Instructions:

1. **Prepare the Guacamole:** In a bowl, mash the avocados and mix with red onion, lime juice, chopped cilantro, salt, and pepper.
2. **Warm the Tortillas:** Heat the tortillas on a griddle or in a dry skillet.
3. **Assemble the Tacos:** Spread a generous amount of guacamole on each tortilla, then top with salsa.
4. **Serve:** Garnish with extra cilantro and serve with lime wedges.

Korean BBQ Beef Tacos with Gochujang Salsa

Ingredients:

- 1 lb thinly sliced beef (such as flank steak or sirloin)
- 1/4 cup soy sauce
- 2 tablespoons brown sugar
- 1 tablespoon sesame oil
- 1 tablespoon garlic (minced)
- 1 tablespoon ginger (minced)
- 1 tablespoon rice vinegar
- 12 small corn tortillas
- 1/2 cup gochujang (Korean chili paste)
- 1/4 cup ketchup
- 1 tablespoon lime juice
- 1/4 cup cilantro (chopped)
- Sesame seeds for garnish

Instructions:

1. **Marinate the Beef:** Combine soy sauce, brown sugar, sesame oil, garlic, ginger, and rice vinegar in a bowl. Add the beef and marinate for at least 30 minutes.
2. **Make the Gochujang Salsa:** In a small bowl, mix gochujang, ketchup, and lime juice.
3. **Cook the Beef:** Grill or pan-fry the marinated beef until cooked to your liking (about 3-4 minutes per side for medium-rare).
4. **Assemble the Tacos:** Warm the tortillas and fill them with the cooked beef. Top with gochujang salsa and garnish with cilantro and sesame seeds.
5. **Serve:** Serve with extra lime wedges.

Salmon Tacos with Cucumber Salsa

Ingredients:

- 2 salmon fillets
- 1 tablespoon olive oil
- 1 teaspoon cumin
- Salt and pepper to taste
- 1 cucumber (diced)
- 1/4 cup red onion (diced)
- 1 tablespoon cilantro (chopped)
- 1 tablespoon lime juice
- 12 small corn tortillas

Instructions:

1. **Cook the Salmon:** Rub the salmon fillets with olive oil, cumin, salt, and pepper. Cook in a hot skillet or grill for 4-5 minutes per side until cooked through.
2. **Prepare the Cucumber Salsa:** Combine diced cucumber, red onion, cilantro, and lime juice in a bowl.
3. **Assemble the Tacos:** Flake the salmon into chunks and fill tortillas with the salmon. Top with cucumber salsa.
4. **Serve:** Serve with extra lime wedges.

Battered Fish Tacos with Chipotle Salsa

Ingredients:

- 1 lb white fish fillets (such as cod or tilapia)
- 1 cup all-purpose flour
- 1/2 teaspoon paprika
- 1/2 teaspoon garlic powder
- Salt and pepper to taste
- 1 cup cold sparkling water
- 12 small corn tortillas
- 1/2 cup chipotle salsa (store-bought or homemade)
- 1/2 cup shredded cabbage
- Lime wedges for garnish

Instructions:

1. **Prepare the Battered Fish:** In a bowl, mix flour, paprika, garlic powder, salt, and pepper. Slowly add sparkling water and whisk to make a batter. Dip fish fillets into the batter, then fry in hot oil (375°F) until golden and crispy, about 3-4 minutes per side.
2. **Assemble the Tacos:** Warm tortillas and fill with the battered fish. Top with chipotle salsa and shredded cabbage.
3. **Serve:** Garnish with lime wedges and serve immediately.

Steak and Avocado Tacos

Ingredients:

- 1 lb flank steak
- 1 tablespoon olive oil
- 1 teaspoon cumin
- 1 teaspoon chili powder
- Salt and pepper to taste
- 1 avocado (sliced)
- 12 small corn tortillas
- 1/4 cup cilantro (chopped)
- Lime wedges for garnish

Instructions:

1. **Cook the Steak:** Rub the steak with olive oil, cumin, chili powder, salt, and pepper. Grill or pan-fry the steak for about 4-5 minutes per side for medium-rare. Let it rest for a few minutes before slicing thinly.
2. **Assemble the Tacos:** Warm the tortillas and fill them with sliced steak and avocado slices.
3. **Serve:** Garnish with chopped cilantro and lime wedges.

Spicy Shrimp Tacos with Pineapple Salsa

Ingredients:

- 1 lb shrimp (peeled and deveined)
- 1 tablespoon olive oil
- 1 teaspoon smoked paprika
- 1/2 teaspoon chili powder
- Salt and pepper to taste
- 1 cup pineapple salsa (pineapple, red onion, cilantro, lime)
- 12 small corn tortillas
- Lime wedges for garnish

Instructions:

1. **Cook the Shrimp:** Toss shrimp in olive oil, paprika, chili powder, salt, and pepper. Sauté in a hot pan for 2-3 minutes per side until pink and cooked through.
2. **Assemble the Tacos:** Warm the tortillas and fill them with the cooked shrimp. Top with pineapple salsa.
3. **Serve:** Garnish with lime wedges and extra cilantro.

Carne Asada Fries with Salsa

Ingredients:

- 1 lb flank steak
- 1 tablespoon olive oil
- 1 teaspoon cumin
- 1 teaspoon garlic powder
- Salt and pepper to taste
- 1 large serving of fries (homemade or frozen)
- 1 cup salsa (your choice of salsa)
- 1/2 cup sour cream
- 1/4 cup cilantro (chopped)

Instructions:

1. **Cook the Carne Asada:** Rub the flank steak with olive oil, cumin, garlic powder, salt, and pepper. Grill or pan-fry for 4-5 minutes per side, then slice thinly.
2. **Prepare the Fries:** Cook the fries according to package directions (or make homemade fries).
3. **Assemble the Carne Asada Fries:** On a large plate, layer the fries, top with sliced carne asada, salsa, and a dollop of sour cream.
4. **Serve:** Garnish with chopped cilantro and serve immediately.

Crispy Fish Tacos with Spicy Avocado Salsa

Ingredients:

- 1 lb white fish fillets (such as cod or tilapia)
- 1 cup all-purpose flour
- 1 teaspoon paprika
- 1/2 teaspoon garlic powder
- Salt and pepper to taste
- 1 cup cold sparkling water
- 12 small corn tortillas
- 1 avocado (mashed)
- 1/2 cup Greek yogurt
- 1 tablespoon lime juice
- 1-2 tablespoons hot sauce (to taste)
- 1/4 cup cilantro (chopped)
- 1/2 cup shredded cabbage

Instructions:

1. **Prepare the Battered Fish:** In a bowl, mix flour, paprika, garlic powder, salt, and pepper. Gradually add sparkling water to create a batter. Dip fish fillets into the batter, then fry in hot oil (375°F) until golden and crispy, about 3-4 minutes per side.
2. **Make the Spicy Avocado Salsa:** Mash the avocado and mix with Greek yogurt, lime juice, hot sauce, and cilantro. Adjust seasoning with salt and pepper.
3. **Assemble the Tacos:** Warm the tortillas and fill with crispy fish. Top with shredded cabbage and drizzle with spicy avocado salsa.
4. **Serve:** Garnish with extra cilantro and lime wedges.

Taco Flatbread with Salsa

Ingredients:

- 4 flatbreads
- 1 cup salsa (your choice of salsa)
- 1 cup shredded cheese (cheddar, mozzarella, or Mexican blend)
- 1/2 cup diced red onion
- 1/2 cup sliced jalapeños
- 1/4 cup chopped cilantro
- 1 tablespoon olive oil

Instructions:

1. **Prepare the Flatbreads:** Preheat your oven to 400°F. Brush each flatbread with olive oil and place on a baking sheet.
2. **Assemble the Flatbreads:** Spread salsa over each flatbread. Sprinkle with shredded cheese, diced onion, and jalapeños.
3. **Bake:** Bake for 8-10 minutes, or until the cheese is melted and bubbly.
4. **Serve:** Garnish with chopped cilantro and serve immediately.

Spicy Chicken Tacos with Mango Habanero Salsa

Ingredients:

- 2 chicken breasts (boneless, skinless)
- 1 tablespoon olive oil
- 1 teaspoon chili powder
- 1 teaspoon cumin
- Salt and pepper to taste
- 1 mango (peeled and diced)
- 1/2 habanero pepper (seeded and finely chopped)
- 1 tablespoon lime juice
- 1/4 cup red onion (diced)
- 12 small corn tortillas

Instructions:

1. **Cook the Chicken:** Rub the chicken breasts with olive oil, chili powder, cumin, salt, and pepper. Grill or pan-fry for 6-8 minutes per side until cooked through. Slice thinly.
2. **Make the Mango Habanero Salsa:** In a bowl, combine diced mango, habanero pepper, lime juice, and red onion. Season with salt.
3. **Assemble the Tacos:** Warm the tortillas and fill with sliced chicken. Top with mango habanero salsa.
4. **Serve:** Garnish with extra lime wedges and serve immediately.

BBQ Pulled Pork Tacos with Cilantro Lime Salsa

Ingredients:

- 2 lbs pork shoulder
- 1 cup BBQ sauce (your favorite brand)
- 1 tablespoon apple cider vinegar
- 1 tablespoon brown sugar
- 12 small corn tortillas
- 1/4 cup cilantro (chopped)
- 1/4 cup red onion (diced)
- 1 tablespoon lime juice
- 1/2 cup sour cream

Instructions:

1. **Cook the Pulled Pork:** Place the pork shoulder in a slow cooker with BBQ sauce, apple cider vinegar, and brown sugar. Cook on low for 6-8 hours, or until the pork is tender and can be easily shredded. Shred the pork using two forks.
2. **Make the Cilantro Lime Salsa:** In a bowl, mix chopped cilantro, red onion, lime juice, and sour cream. Season with salt and pepper.
3. **Assemble the Tacos:** Warm the tortillas and fill with pulled pork. Top with cilantro lime salsa.
4. **Serve:** Garnish with extra cilantro and serve immediately.

Grilled Veggie Tacos with Corn Salsa

Ingredients:

- 1 zucchini (sliced)
- 1 bell pepper (sliced)
- 1 red onion (sliced)
- 1 tablespoon olive oil
- Salt and pepper to taste
- 1 cup corn kernels (fresh or frozen)
- 1/4 cup diced red onion
- 1/4 cup cilantro (chopped)
- 1 tablespoon lime juice
- 12 small corn tortillas

Instructions:

1. **Grill the Veggies:** Toss zucchini, bell pepper, and onion with olive oil, salt, and pepper. Grill for 5-7 minutes per side until tender and slightly charred.
2. **Make the Corn Salsa:** In a bowl, combine corn, diced red onion, cilantro, and lime juice. Season with salt and pepper.
3. **Assemble the Tacos:** Warm the tortillas and fill with grilled veggies. Top with corn salsa.
4. **Serve:** Garnish with extra cilantro and serve immediately.

Tex-Mex Tacos with Roasted Pepper Salsa

Ingredients:

- 1 lb ground beef or turkey
- 1 tablespoon taco seasoning
- 12 small flour tortillas
- 1 red bell pepper (roasted and diced)
- 1 yellow bell pepper (roasted and diced)
- 1/4 cup diced onion
- 1 tablespoon lime juice
- 1/4 cup cilantro (chopped)

Instructions:

1. **Cook the Meat:** Brown the ground beef or turkey in a skillet over medium heat, breaking it apart with a spoon. Add taco seasoning and cook according to package directions.
2. **Make the Roasted Pepper Salsa:** Roast the bell peppers until the skin is charred, then peel and dice. Combine the roasted peppers with diced onion, lime juice, and chopped cilantro. Season with salt and pepper.
3. **Assemble the Tacos:** Warm the tortillas and fill with seasoned meat. Top with roasted pepper salsa.
4. **Serve:** Garnish with extra cilantro and serve immediately.

www.ingramcontent.com/pod-product-compliance
Lightning Source LLC
LaVergne TN
LVHW081505060526
838201LV00056BA/2939